Kilroy, James
James Clarence Mangan

James Clarence Mangan

THE IRISH WRITERS SERIES

James F. Carens, General Editor

TITLE	AUTHOR
Sean O'Casey	Bernard Benstock
J. C. Mangan	James Kilroy
W. R. Rodgers	Darcy O'Brien
Standish O'Grady	Phillip L. Marcus
Austin Clarke	John Jordan
Brian Friel	D. E. S. Maxwell
Daniel Corkery	George Brandon Saul
Eimar O'Duffy	Robert Hogan
Frank O'Connor	James Matthews
George Moore	Janet Egleson
James Joyce	Fritz Senn
John Butler Yeats	Douglas Archibald
Lord Edward Dunsany	Zack Bowen
Maria Edgeworth	James Newcomer
Mary Lavin	Zack Bowen
Oscar Wilde	Edward Partridge
Paul Vincent Carroll	Paul A. Doyle
Seumas O'Kelly	George Brandon Saul
Sheridan LeFanu	Michael Begnal
Somerville and Ross	John Cronin
Susan Mitchell	Richard M. Kain
J. M. Synge	Robin Skelton
Katharine Tynan	Marilyn Gaddis Rose
Liam O'Flaherty	James O'Brien
Iris Murdoch	Donna Gerstenberger

JAMES CLARENCE MANGAN

by
James Kilroy

Lewisburg
BUCKNELL UNIVERSITY PRESS

Associated University Presses, Inc.
Cranbury, New Jersey 08512

ISBN: 0-8387-7617-5 paper edition
0-8387-7749-X cloth edition
Printed in the United States of America

Contents

Contents

Chronology of J. C. Mangan

Very little is known of Mangan's life. He lived and died in seclusion; his life was short and unhappy. Although he published scores of poems under various pseudonyms, only one book-length volume appeared in his lifetime. Because of all this, the following chronology is of necessity brief.

May 1, 1803	Born in Dublin.
1813	Began apprenticeship as scrivener.
1818	First poems published under various pseudonyms.
1832–33	Contributor to *The Comet*.
1834–49	Contributor to *Dublin University Magazine*.
1838	Began work for Irish Ordnance Survey.
Oct. 15, 1842	First issue of *The Nation*, includes Mangan poems.
1844	Asst. cataloguer at Trinity College Library.
1845	*Anthologia Germanica*—only volume of work in lifetime.
June 20, 1849	Died in Dublin.

James Clarence Mangan

I

If the name of James Clarence Mangan is known,
it is so often because both James Joyce and W. B. Yeats
regarded him as a major writer of the previous century
and mentioned him in their works. And if the modern
reader's knowledge of Mangan extends to an acquain-
tance with his works, inevitably the legend of Mangan's
miserable life and the music of his poetry merge, so
that he visualizes Mangan, the Man in the Cloak. In
many ways Mangan is unique: one of the most gifted,
but the strangest and most tormented of Irish writers.
But at the same time it must be remarked that more
than any other poet of the nineteenth century, and
probably more than any poet since then as well, Mangan
represents Ireland, and the suffering of his life can be
seen as symbolizing the miseries of his country in the
middle of the last century.

In his own land, he is by no means forgotten. "Dark
Rosaleen," his best-known poem, is still subjected to
recitations and quoted on any number of occasions.
But outside of Ireland, he is remembered only for a
half dozen anthology pieces which are included in all
representative collections of Irish verse. The only fairly

comprehensive editions of his works, the two by D. J. O'Donoghue which were published in 1903 and 1904, are long out of print and have become collector's items. But in his lifetime Mangan composed a huge number of poems, as well as reviews, stories and essays. Because he wrote under a number of pseudonyms, attribution has been difficult; but in the last several years, real progress has been made in determining what contributions to the *Dublin University Magazine* and other periodicals may be ascribed to him. It is to be hoped that before long a more complete and more scholarly edition of his works can be made available.

One peculiarity of Mangan which has attracted, and in certain cases repelled, readers is his love of word play. His urge to pun and to attempt challenging or even preposterous rhymes simply could not be controlled. So it is true that in some of his most serious poems or most intriguing stories, there are jokes or distracting musical effects. But counterweighed against these are the painful, strong subjects of his best compositions. Particularly in his patriotic poems, Mangan speaks with conviction and even passion, so that at times some relief in comedy is helpful.

Before proceeding to a consideration of Mangan's translations, original poems and prose works, it is well to recount the strange story of his life.

Biographical information on Mangan is by now relatively inaccessible; D. J. O'Donoghue's book-length biography appeared in 1897, and the few subsequent studies of his life have added little to that book.[1] And

---

1. See Rudolph Patrick Holzapfel, *James Clarence Mangan, A Check List of Printed and Other Sources* (Dublin: Scepter Books, 1969) for a complete check list of critical studies.

Mangan's life was so strange and so tortured that it remains in the reader's mind and becomes almost a legend. The poet himself contributed to mystifying his critics by mythologizing his own childhood and early life in the version he included in the published fragment of his *Autobiography*. The result is that Mangan's life can be read as a parable of the damned poet, alienated, lonesome and driven nearly to madness by his poetic vision and sensitive nature.

James Mangan (the Clarence was his later addition) was born on May 1, 1803, at Number 3 Fishamble Street, Dublin—in the very oldest part of the city. There he was to spend the rest of his life. One of the many uncanny coincidences relating him to Edgar Allan Poe was the fact that the house in which he was born had until the eighteenth century been owned by the Ussher family, whose coat of arms were still on the outside wall. His father had been a teacher before marrying Catherine Smith and taking over the grocery shop she had inherited. Mangan liked to remark on the fact that Thomas Moore was also a grocer's son, and was born, a generation earlier, within easy walking distance of Fishamble Street. But the elder James Mangan was not the warm and respectable man that Moore's father was. The poet described him as having a "calm concentrated spirit of Milesian fierceness," not fitted for business and irresponsible. To his family he was tyrannous:

Me, my two brothers, and my sister, he treated habitually as a huntsman would treat refractory hounds. It was his boast, uttered in pure glee of heart, that we 'would run into a mouse-hole' to shun him. While my mother

lived he made her miserable—he led my only sister such
a life that she was obliged to leave our house—he kept
up a succession of continual hostilities with my brothers
—and if he spared me more than others it was perhaps
because I displayed a greater contempt of life and every-
thing connected with it than he thought was shown by
the other members of his family. If any one can imagine
such an idea as a human boa-constrictor *without his
alimentive propensities* he will be able to form some
notion of the character of my father.

Because of the father's own improvidence, his grocery
business and all the other commercial ventures he attempted failed. As debts piled up his family suffered
not only from poverty but from his mounting irasci-
bility and frustrations. What seems to have affected
Clarence most severely was the irreligious atmosphere
of his home: "I . . . came into the world surrounded . . .
by an atmosphere of curses and intemperance, of cruelty,
infidelity and blasphemy—and of both secret and open
hatred towards the moral government of GOD—such
as few infants, on opening their eyes to the first light
of day had ever known before."

As a result of the ill treatment and neglect, he "sought
refuge in books and solitude." So complete was his isola-
tion from his family that by the age of fourteen, they
called him "mad," and he afterwards claimed that during these early years, "the seeds of that moral insanity
were developed within me which afterwards grew up
into a tree of giant altitude."

He was sent to school, where he received special
attention from a few teachers who recognized his
genius. He was taught the rudiments of Latin, French,
Spanish and Italian; but the extent of his knowledge of

these and other languages is questionable, particularly since he was only educated to the age of fifteen. In school, as throughout his life, he enjoyed no close friendships or even real involvement with others. It was not merely that he was shy; he wrote:

> I merely felt or fancied that between me and those who approached me no species of sympathy could exist; and I shrank from communion with them as from somewhat alien from my nature. This feeling continued to acquire strength daily, until in after years it became one of the grand and terrible miseries of my existence. It was a morbid product of the pride and presumption which, almost hidden from myself, constituted even from my childhood, governing traits in my character, and have so often contributed to render me repulsive in the eyes of others.

To support his family, he left school at age fifteen to become an apprentice to a scrivener, a position he hated but endured for three years, working from dawn until nearly midnight, until one day he collapsed and was hospitalized. He had begun writing poetry by this time, and in his *Autobiography* he quotes a poem, "Genius," composed when he was sixteen. As expected, the poem reveals his discontent and melancholy, but it also states his recognition of his own role as a man of genius—endowed differently and cursed by his gifts as well as by the world that cannot understand him.

During his hospitalization, Mangan claimed, he contracted "an incurable hypochondriasis," by exposure to a young boy who had leprosy. That this ailment of his was not actual leprosy is generally accepted, but whether it was dyspepsia associated with his dominating melancholy or a mental imbalance cannot be ascertained. Actual physical disorders did continue to plague him, and more than once he collapsed.

When he returned to work in the scrivener's office, and later as an attorney's clerk, the responsibilities of supporting his family and his disdain for his coarse and vulgar fellow workers again drove him to despair and near insanity:

> I seemed to myself to be shut up in a cavern with serpents and scorpions and all hideous and monstrous things, which writhed and hissed around me, and discharged their slime and venom over my person. These hallucinations were considerably aided and aggravated by the pestiferous atmosphere of the office, the chimney of which smoked continually, and for some hours before the close of the day emitted a sulphurous exhalation that at times literally caused me to gasp for breath. In a word I felt utterly and thoroughly miserable.

Religious despair followed and he seemed close to suicide. But throughout this period he was educating himself, by reading widely and writing poetry. It must have been around this time that his addiction to either opium or alcohol began. D. J. O'Donoghue claimed that Mangan began taking opium to relieve the constant pain of his various ailments; others, such as Mangan's friend Charles Gavan Duffy, have claimed that Mangan was only an alcoholic. But whatever escape he sought, his addiction further damaged his health and caused a problem that continued for the rest of his life. In one of his letters, he admits some such addiction; speaking of his suffering as an attorney's clerk, he writes: "In seeking to escape from this misery I had lain the foundation of that evil habit which has since proved so ruinous to me."

An unhappy love affair, the details of which have puzzled subsequent critics, further damaged his confidence. But by then he had begun publishing his poems, and some loose association with Dublin literary circles began. His first poems appeared as early as 1818, when he was only fifteen. Under various pseudonyms, as unlikely as "Peter Puff," "M. E.," "P. V. McGuffin," and many others, he began to publish poetry regularly. By 1832 and 1833 some of his best poems were appearing in *The Comet*, a Dublin paper of the time which had as its main cause the opposition to laws requiring tithes from Catholics to pay for Protestant clergy. In submitting work to this paper, Mangan joined some of the established writers of Ireland, such as Thomas Browne, John Sheehan and Maurice O'Connell (Daniel's son) ; but he remained aloof from them, and grew even more eccentric in his appearance. Outside, he usually wore a cloak and a strange high hat; he probably wore a wig, although on that matter there is irrelevant disagreement. In his bizarre manner of dress, he resembles one of his admitted heroes, the Dublin writer Charles Robert Maturin. The author of *Melmoth the Wanderer*, who died in 1824, also dressed oddly—in practically the same manner as Mangan, right down to the cloak. Certainly influence of Maturin's most famous novel is evident in Mangan's works, particularly in two stories, "The Man in the Cloak," and "The Thirty Flasks."

By the mid-1830s, Mangan had contributed pieces to *The Comet, The Dublin Penny Journal* and *The*

Satirist. In 1834, he began submitting work to the *Dublin University Magazine.* For the rest of his life, he contributed hundreds of poems and prose pieces to this important periodical, which also featured works by such well-known writers as Samuel Lover, Charles Lever, Sheridan Le Fanu, William Carleton and Samuel Ferguson, the major Irish writers of this time. His contributions ranged from translations from the German to imitations of Eastern poetry and fantasies. To supplement his income he worked as a tutor of German for a while. In 1838 he was employed by the Ordnance Survey, serving as a copyist under George Petrie, John O'Donovan and Eugene O'Curry. The association with these three eminent scholars encouraged him in investigating Irish learning; all three had been involved in making copies and extracts of Irish manuscripts, and are credited with rediscovering the Irish cultural heritage at this time. As part of his work for the Ordnance Survey, Mangan did research in Marsh's Library and Trinity College library. A contemporary account of him in the last-named place well describes Mangan's appearance:

> Being in the college library, and having occasion for a book in that gloomy apartment of the institution called the "Fagel Library," which is the innermost recess of the stately building, an acquaintance pointed out to me a man perched on the top of a ladder, with the whispered information that the figure was Clarence Mangan. It was an unearthly and ghostly figure, in a brown garment; the same garment (to all appearance) which lasted till the day of his death. The blanched hair was totally unkempt; the corpse-like features still as marble; a large book was in his arms, and all his soul was in the book. I had never

heard of Clarence Mangan before, and knew not for what he was celebrated; whether as a magician, a poet, or a murderer; yet took a volume and spread it on a table, not to read, but with pretence of reading to gaze on the spectral creature upon the ladder.[2]

Mangan experimented widely with new verse forms and exotic subjects, and was remarkably playful and irreverent in his writings. But the business of literature was a serious vocation nevertheless. He wrote, at one point, "No luxuriance of imagination can atone for the absence of perspicuity. A poet above all men should endeavour to make words the images of things." And elsewhere he commented, "The best poetry is that which most resembles the best prose." His translations of German and Irish poems are among his most successful poems, although at times they are inexact and even range so far from the originals as to more properly be called "versions," rather than "translations." In fact, Mangan knew little Irish; most of the actual translation was done by others, Eugene O'Curry principally.

In October 1842 *The Nation* first appeared. It had been founded by Charles Gavan Duffy, Thomas Davis and John Blake Dillon; Duffy served as its editor. The Young Ireland Movement, of which this newspaper was the organ, was not the most effective political group of Irish history, but it was certainly a dynamic and influential one, in that it so encouraged asserting a unique national identity, and awakening interest in Ireland's heritage in its art and literature, that its effects are still evident. Although Mangan published a poem in its first

---

2. John Mitchel, "Introduction" to D. J. O'Donoghue edition, *Poems of James Clarence Mangan* (Dublin: M. H. Gill, 1903), pp. xxxiv-v.

issue, "*The Nation*'s First Number," he only infrequently submitted poems to this newspaper before the last few years of his life, when he turned to composing patriotic verse primarily.

Despite his lack of interest in political affairs in the early forties, his poetic powers were recognized by even the most active politicians. Charles Gavan Duffy and Thomas Davis tried to get Mangan's poems published in London, but failed. Later, when his *Anthologia Germanica* was published in Dublin, it was Duffy who financed the project.

By 1846, when the potato famine was underway, and until his death in 1849, a more serious and nationalistic poetry predominates. His best remembered poems, "Dark Rosaleen," "A Vision of Connaught in the Thirteenth Century," and "The Warning Voice," all appeared in *The Nation* in these last years.

For all his mature life, Mangan continued to suffer from ill health, loneliness and addiction. His closest friend of his last years, the Reverend C. P. Meehan, ministered to him as best he could, but eventually Mangan died alone, and nearly unknown. A cholera epidemic swept Dublin in 1849, and on June 20 of that year he died in the Meath Hospital in his native city. Whether the actual cause of death was cholera or malnutrition remains in dispute. A haunting pencil drawing of the dead Mangan done by Sir Frederick Burton survives, in the collection of the National Gallery of Ireland.

Mangan was buried in Glasnevin Cemetery, where many of Ireland's great men are laid, but his funeral was nearly ignored: only five people attended, due to the epidemic still raging, and, of course, to his life-long withdrawal from society.

Although he was interested in exotic religions and philosophies, including Oriental teachings and the writings of Swedenborg, Mangan remained a constant and even devout Catholic. His *Autobiography*, with its explicit intention of moral instruction and frequent allusions to God ("GOD is *the* idea of my mind.") indicates the religious fervor of his last years.

But by the end he welcomed death, if only as an escape from constant physical suffering. In an autobiographical fragment published after his death, he had written:

> I have long felt that this human world had died to me. The lights and shadows of life's picture had long since been blended into one chaos of dense and indistinguishable blackness. The pilgrimage of my blank years pointed across a desert where flower or green thing was forbidden to live, and it mattered not how soon some shifting column of sand descended and swept me into its bosom. Thereafter darkness would swathe my memory for ever. Not one poor sigh would be expended for me. No hands would care to gather mine unremembered ashes into the sanctuary of an urn. Of what cared I then if those who attempted to break down with their feeble fingers the adamantine barrier that severed me from a communion with mankind, perceiving the futility of their enterprise, retired from my presence with disgust and despair?[3]

*   *   *   *   *

Establishing the context in which to view a writer such as Mangan is not an easy task. With whom should

---

3. *The Evening Packet* (11 October 1849), p. 3383.

he be compared, and in what category of authors may he be placed?

Mangan was born in Dublin in 1803, and until his death in 1849 probably never left the city and its suburbs. The subjects of most of his poems are Irish, but he cannot be simply discounted as a provincial writer, because of his remarkable knowledge of foreign literature and his translations from various languages, particularly of the German romantic poets. Reference to some of his favorite German models is helpful, and one can find striking similarities in the works and even biography of Friedrich Rückert, for instance. But there are other sides to Mangan revealed in his original poems and prose works; his intense love of Ireland must be taken into account.

He contributed to *The Nation,* and shared with the members of the Young Ireland movement much of the romantic nationalism, inspired by Mazzini and the revolutionary movements on the Continent. Some of his best poems bewail Ireland's suffering and sing of hope for her independence. Thomas Davis and Charles Gavan Duffy were friends of his, and his benefactors as well; he shared their ideals and felt sorrow at the defeat of the Young Ireland group in its unsuccessful attempt at revolution in 1848. But one has only to thumb through the widely popular collection, *The Spirit of the Nation,* still in print after over fifty editions, to realize Mangan's preeminence. Davis, Duffy, "Speranza" (Oscar Wilde's mother) , and the other contributors were experts at propaganda, "Poster art" as Padraic Fallon termed it, having wide appeal and a real use during the ıevolutionary times in which it was written. Mangan shared some of their qualities, but in his best patriotic poems there is more—a theme not limited to a single time or occasion, and a music which continues to evoke strong reactions more than a century later.

Certain of Mangan's other compatriots present suggestive parallels. He mentions the common background he shared with Thomas Moore; but for all of Moore's trade in Irish songs, he has not the patriotic fervor of Mangan, nor are his interests in foreign literature, as embodied in *Lallah Rookh*, as interesting to modern readers as Mangan's versions of German writers. The Gothic novelist Charles Robert Maturin shares personal eccentricities with Mangan, and sure influence is evidenced in Mangan's "The Man in the Cloak." But again the parallel is limited, particularly in the last years of Mangan's life, when he became involved in political causes. Another Irishman, Francis Mahony, who wrote under the name "Father Prout," was born in Cork only a year after Mangan. Both men indulged in literary pranks, particularly in bogus translations. And Mahony's best-known poem, "The Bells of Shandon," echoes the strong rhymes and rhythms of Mangan's verse. But *The Reliques of Father Prout* reveal the classical and religious concerns of the ordained Jesuit, and practically none of the national pride of Mangan's works. Joseph Sheridan LeFanu, the author of *Uncle Silas*, comes to mind, at least in his interest in the Gothic and supernatural, which he shares with Mangan. Such comparison is more appropriate than the others in some ways, but the humor and variety of

Mangan is not matched in the younger fellow-Dubliner.

Despite the fact that he never submitted poems or stories to papers outside of Ireland, Mangan does exhibit qualities of his contemporaries across the Irish Sea. We tend to overlook the fact that Keats was only eight years older than Mangan, and Tennyson only six years younger. Their experiments in verse forms and techniques, although not real influences, do indicate the kind of literary activity current at the time. And the heady atmosphere of their lyric poems does find some parallel in Mangan's verse, even though he did not achieve the artistry of their best poems. The bizarre humor of Thomas Hood's poetry may be recalled in reading some of Mangan's verse. Equally noteworthy is the similarity of Mangan to an English poet who is an exact contemporary; Thomas Lovell Beddoes was born and died in the same years as Mangan. He shared some Irish heritage, being the nephew of Maria Edgeworth, and was, like Mangan, a student of German literature. But most striking are their similar literary effects. Beddoe's *Death's Jest-Book* was once termed "florid Gothic in poetry," a description which fits some of Mangan as well. Both men combine in their works a concentration on the subject of death with humorous treatment.

But the similarity most often commented upon, and the one most revealing in analysis, is that between Mangan and Edgar Allan Poe. The American writer was only six years younger than Mangan and died just three months after him. In a number of details their lives paralleled each other, particularly in their common alcoholism and possible use of opium. Both took up poetry at an early age, and the published pieces of their juvenalia reveal exceptional talents. Although his childhood was happier than Mangan's, by age eighteen Poe saw his life as miserable, and saw no reason to hope for solace for his "sear'd and blighted heart." Extreme melancholy marred both their lives and both died young.

However, the similarities in their lives lead us only to comment on coincidences. More relevant and more surprising are the similarities in their works. The best-known poems of each exhibit poetic experiments almost identical. The internal rhymes, strong alliterative elements, conscious assonance and onomotopoeia, and striking rhythm of "The Raven" find a parallel, in 1845, the time of its appearance, only in the poems of Mangan. So, too, the cadences of "Dark Rosaleen" and "To Laura," as well as their language and imagery, recall Poe.

Critics have concentrated their attention on two main points of similarity: the use by both Mangan and Poe of two peculiar poetic techniques. Both employ internal rhymes to an exceptional degree. Mangan, in his translation of Gottfried Burger's "Lenore," written in 1834, uses it often, even though it is almost absent in the original German. In other poems of this period, it also appears, and he continued to use it throughout his career. Poe's extensive use of internal rhyme began later. His "Lenore" (coincidences of this sort abound) was first published in 1831 as "A Paean," but it was so revised in later printings that the early version hardly resembles the final poem. By 1843, the version printed in *The Pioneer* is much closer to Mangan's verse in its rhythm and other sound effects. By 1845, short lines have been combined into longer ones, which results in consistent use of internal rhyme, much like that found in Mangan's poem "The Sorrows of Innisfail."

The other poetic technique both favor is the use of the refrain, particularly of a special type, in which the repeated phrase changes in slight but cumulative ways with each repetition. Mangan's translation of Goethe's "Mignon" illustrates the technique so clearly employed in "The Raven." Although Poe claimed originality for the structure of this, his most famous poem, it is not so different from a number of earlier poems by his Irish contemporary.

In their prose, the similarities are not striking, except in Poe's very earliest pieces, such as "The Duc De L'Omelette," which has a wild verbal humor and taste for the diabolic that we find also in Mangan's "The Thirty Flasks."

Based on these and other similarities, the question of direct influence has inevitably been raised. Francis J. Thompson has recently argued that Mangan was influenced by Poe, particularly by *Tamerlane*, which appeared in 1827, and could well have been circulated in Dublin during Mangan's early career. His namesake, however, the English poet who died in 1907, felt that the influence was equally certain, but that it went in the other direction: "The *Dublin University Magazine* was well known to American journalists; and Poe took suggestions as a cat laps milk, although he made his own what he took." In 1916 Thomas MacDonagh called Poe "a student of Mangan," and at least one doctoral dissertation, that of Henry Edward Cain which was submitted to the Catholic University of America in 1929, has examined the subject of influence between Poe and Mangan.

The result of such investigation has not been conclusive, however. Similarities there certainly are: remarkable agreement in attitudes and almost identical practices in certain poems; but direct influence still seems unlikely—either from or to Mangan.

Both Poe and Mangan reflect the milieu of the middle nineteenth century—its revolutionary unrest, its sense of injustices and yet its confusion at the rapid changes of those years. In literary accomplishments, they are exceptional in the *extent* of the experimentation with technique which they both undertook, but not in the *type* of endeavor. Tennyson, for one, was also attempting new structural arrangements and unusual sound effects in his poetry at this time. Both Mangan and Poe built on the poetry of the romantic period, and echoes of Keats, Byron and Coleridge occur regularly. Cain argues that Coleridge's influence on both poets was most substantial, and that it accounts for some of the most startling similarities noted. As is seen in Maturin, Beddoes or any number of writers of this time, the taste for the grotesque or exotic was not confined to these two writers. In short, they share attitudes, goals and even poetic practices to a great extent, but neither seems to have directly influenced the other in any definite way. This does not deny the equally apparent differences

seen in their works. Without any doubt, Poe uses natural details and exercises imagination much more skil-
fully. But equally indisputable is the greater fervor of
Mangan and the emotional force of the best of his
poems, particularly those on political subjects.

Mangan was in many ways a man of the nineteenth
century; he certainly was a man of Ireland. But com-
parisons fail to account for the singular effects of the
poetry and even his prose.

II

It is in his translations that the genius of Mangan most forcefully strikes the modern reader. It was by these poems that he was best known in his lifetime; his only book published while he lived was the *Anthologia Germanica,* which appeared in 1845. This anthology consisted of his translations of German poetry previously published in the *Dublin University Magazine* and in other Irish periodicals. Along with German poems, he published versions of Irish poems, posthumously published in John O'Daly's *The Poets and Poetry of Munster*, and a great number of poems based on Spanish and verse of the Islamic countries. D. J. O'Donoghue, in his edition of Mangan's poems—still the most complete and representative collection even though it prints only about one-fifth of Mangan's total output—includes more than twice as many translations as original poems. But subsequent critics have agreed with that choice, arguing that the translations as a whole constitute Mangan's best poetry. Francis Thompson, who exhibits some of Mangan's techniques and attitudes in his own poetry, commented, Mangan "needed a suggestion or a model to set his genius working."

Mangan's knowledge of several languages is testified to by even the scant biographical information that has survived. He was particularly fluent in German and worked as a tutor in that language for a short while. He reportedly was educated in several other languages—Latin, French and Italian—and made some progress later in his life in mastering Irish. But it is unlikely that he had any knowledge of a number of the languages which he pretended to translate: Welsh, Frisian, Bohemian, Danish or the various Islamic tongues, Arabic, Turkish and Persian. His poems claiming to be translations of these languages were probably based on recent translations, of which there were a sufficient number during the 1830s and 1840s. Islamic influences were particularly strong at this time. In literature it is evidenced by Thomas Moore's *Lallah Rookh* and the tremendous popularity of Byron's oriental poems, one of which sold 10,000 copies on the first day of its issue. The pseudo-Turkish pavillion at Brighton and the rather amusing versions of Turkish harems in painting, reveal the taste for the mysterious and exotic Orient that existed in Regency and early Victorian England, as well as in Ireland.

Mangan's irreverence to the originals can easily be overstated. One has only to look at Mangan's contemporary poet and fellow Irishman, Francis Mahony ("Father Prout") to see a playful treatment of translations, not uncommon at the time. For reasons no more noble than sheer dislike and revenge, Mahony published "The Rogueries of Tom Moore," in which he quotes Greek, Latin and Old French versions of

Moore's poems. He claimed these to be the originals from which Moore plagiarized—all made up by Mahony, of course. The parallels between these two Irish poets are suggestive: the one lived in obscurity in Dublin and published his poetry only in Irish periodicals; the other left Cork and lived on the Continent most of his life, associating with the Fraserians and the literary set of London, and the Brownings and others in Florence and Rome. The Latin and French translations in *The Reliques of Father Prout* remind us of Mangan's in their strong rhythms and departures from the originals. And Mahony's best-remembered poem, "The Bells of Shandon," certainly exhibits the sound effects of Mangan's verse, particularly its use of onomotopoeia and feminine rhymes. Both men led unhappy lives, ending in lonely deaths. Although they were born only a year apart, Mahony lived on until 1866; he died in Paris and his body was brought back to Ireland to be buried in his native Cork. The humor and irreverence of both poets only glazes over the religious fervor and suffering of both of their lives.

Of his translations, Mangan's German poems are the most lyrical. In them he departs quite often from the strict phrasing, rhymes and metrical schemes of the originals, but succeeds, in many instances, in capturing their spirit and sentiment.

In "Noon-day Dreaming," his translation of Wilhelm Müller's "Wohin?" Mangan preserves the three-stress line of the original, and adds rhyme to every line, rather than to alternate lines only. But in many other poems, his version has less similarity to the original. "Where's

My Money," a translation of Franz Baron von Gaudy's "Wo Bleibt's?," has the same number of stanzas as the German poem, and its argument follows the same general course. But the English poem has a lot of familiar Mangan: jokes about drinking and complaints about the meagre pay he received for magazine contributions. In other words, Mangan adds ideas and metaphors to the point that the original poems become the scaffolding for a new poem. Sometimes this remodelling results in a poem better than the original; the poem entitled "Song" is better in Mangan's version than in the German "Lebenspflichten" by Ludwig Holty. Building on a simple *carpe diem* theme, Mangan added sensuous imagery and achieved a much more melancholy tone. But the Irish poet's tendency to excess mars some of the poems too. In "Ichabod! Thy Glory Has Departed," based on Ludwig Uhland's "Nachtreise," he keeps close to the original in structure and content, even to maintaining the same rhyme scheme. But then he overstates the conclusion. The central irony of old age and time stealing the joy of life is evident from the start, but in Mangan's last stanza he so belabors it that the whole poem is compromised:

> But the gold of the sunshine is shed and gone
> And the once bright roses are dead and wan,
>   And my love in her low grave moulders,
> And I ride through a dark, dark land by night
> With never a star to bless me with light,
>   And the Mantle of Age on my shoulders.

In his translations of poems by Ludwig Tieck, Mangan captures much of the strong music and vivid colors of the originals. The German poet's conscious experimentation with sounds and his use of exaggerated, even grotesque, imagery find expression in the Irish poet's verse also.

Mangan's translations of the three major German romantic poets, Goethe, Schiller and Heine, are less successful. Heine's delicate style and subtle variations of meter elude Mangan. Schiller and Goethe are better treated, but Mangan seems almost intimidated by the originals. He maintains the original rhyme scheme and content of "The Violet" by Goethe, for instance, but only at the expense of employing painful contractions ("vi'let"), and awkward twisting of syntax. He translated more poems by Schiller than any other poet, and these are not slavish translations. But they are not successful poems either; Mangan never achieves the detail and strong visual qualities of his German master.

It is in translating the poems of Rückert and Kerner that Mangan excels. The musical quality achieved by the strong rhythm and clear rhymes of the English poems are entirely evocative of the originals. "And Then No More," based on a poem by Friedrich Rückert, is generally regarded as one of Mangan's best poems. Its first stanza illustrates the elaborate rhymes and sound effects of the poem:

I saw her once, one little while, and then no more:
'Twas Eden's light on Earth awhile, and then no more.
Amid the throng she passed along the meadow floor:
Spring seemed to smile on Earth awhile, and then no more;
But whence she came, which way she went, what garb she
    wore
I noted not; I gazed awhile, and then no more.

The single end rhyme is contained throughout four stanzas, as is the internal rhyme on "while." But there are other internal rhymes (throng/along; smile/awhile) and frequent instances of assonance and alliteration (Amid/meadow; whence/which/went/what; noted/not). The deliberate placing of caesurae to achieve varying effects strikes us: two pauses in the first, fifth and sixth lines break the line into three distinct units. In the second and fourth lines, the break divides it into two uneven parts. And, in the third line, no pause is indicated, although the dominant rhythm and the internal rhyme suggest a pair of subtle pauses. In various details Mangan's similarities to Rückert are striking, and it is likely that some of the Irish poet's interest in Oriental poetry comes from his German contemporary, who became the most important German translator and scholar of Oriental verse of his time. Like Mangan he was fascinated by experiments with sound in verse, particularly in unusual rhymes. In "Gone in the Wind" and "Nature More Than Science," Mangan's translations of two other poems by Rückert, similar uses of rhyme and sounds are apparent.

Justinus Kerner was another of Mangan's favorites. He, too, was a contemporary, and had achieved some fame as a doctor with his observations of the "Ghost-seeress of Prevorst." With those investigations of the supernatural, Mangan was undoubtedly fascinated, as is indicated by his two versions of Kerner's poems to that woman. The air of melancholy in such poems as "The Poet's Consolation" found accurate expression in Mangan's translations. "The Saw-Mill," which D. J. O'Donoghue subtitles only "from the German," seems a very free translation of "Wanderer in der Sägemuhle" by Kerner.

In general, Mangan's peculiarities as a poet—his experiments with rhyme and other sound effects, his interest in the mystical and his over-riding gloom—all equip him for translation of his German contemporaries. But in the best poems of this category, he is not literal in his translation: usually he adds to the originals, and at his worst he shows off, by excessive use of elaborate rhymes or strange meters suggested by the original poems.

On at least one technical matter he found German a most compatible language, sometimes too compatible. He noted that the infinitive of most German verbs is a polysyllabic, ending in "en"; this ending occurs in many other verbs as well, and so double-rhymes are frequent. Mangan's own use of feminine rhymes and even triple rhymes is so common as to become distracting in his worst poems.

* * *

Mangan's poems based on literature of the Islamic languages are difficult to assess as translations. He began as early as 1837 to publish "Literae Orientales" in the *Dublin University Magazine*, and published a good number of these "versions" for the next few years. His biographers agree that he must have known none of the Oriental languages, but got them from contemporary translations, particularly those of Rückert. And it is likely that some of the professed translations are original poems, just as those attributed to the German "Selber" seem to have been Mangan's own.

The Oriental poems well illustrate Mangan's skill

in experimenting with unusual metrical and rhyme
schemes. "The Time Ere the Roses Were Blowing"
Mangan attributes to Kazem Zerbayeh, a sixteenth-
century Persian poet. The first stanza shows the poem's
elaborate metrical scheme and strong rhyme:

> Brillantly sparkle, Meseehi, thy flowing
> Numbers, like streams amid lilies upgrowing,
> Yet, wouldst thou mingle the sad and sublime,
>   Sing, too, the Time,
> Sing the young Time *ere* the Roses were blowing!

The dactyllic trimeter lines are short and fast-moving.
The feminine rhyme is insistent in three of the five lines.
The third line, which has one less syllable than the
other long lines, rhymes with the next line, but the
first syllable of that line, that which would complete the
third, is the "ing" rhyme. Internal rhymes occur again
("sparkle" and "mingle") and the rhythm is varied,
particularly in the last line. The effect of the marked
emphasis of the last line is to make it symmetrical both
with the first couplet and with the fourth line: "Sing,
too, the Time, . . . Sing the young Time."

"The Angel of Death: A Persian Legend" has a more
involved stanzaic structure, as seen in the first two
stanzas:

> Great Zuleimaun was King of Kings.
>   He ruled o'er Deevs and men.
>   For him had Allah's hand updrawn
> The veil that shrouds all mystic things.
>   On Earth shall reign agen
>   No King like Zuleimaun!
>
> He sate within his Council-room
>   One morn in Summer-time,

> And held high converse with Azreel,
> The Messenger of Death and Doom,
> On Fate, and Good, and Crime,
> And future woe and weal:

The first two lines are written in iambic tetrameter and iambic trimeter, a familiar sequence in a narrative poem such as this. But the next two lines, which also form a unit, are both iambic tetrameter, and the last two go back to trimeter again. Thus, the slowest statement is that made in the middle two lines, particularly in line four, the most stressed line. But in counterpoint to this division into three couplets, the rhyme scheme divides the stanza into two triplets; thus the stanza is short enough, and the rhyme dominant, so that a strong close of each stanza is achieved.

"The Time of the Barmecides" was reportedly Mangan's favorite of his own poems. Here the measure alternates between four stresses and three stresses per line. But although the general measure is iambic, there are so many variations of meter as to make it closer to accentual verse:

> Then Youth was mine, and a fierce wild will,
> And an iron arm in war,
> And a fleet foot high upon Ishkar's hill,
> When the watch-lights glimmered afar, . . .

Although the lines do not scan neatly, the rhythm is strong—perhaps too dominant for a narrative poem. Such unusual rhythms were identified with Mangan, and are skillfully parodied in the following anonymous verse, published during his lifetime:

Various and curious are thy strains, O Clarence Mangan,
Rhyming and chiming in a very odd way.
Rhyming and chiming! and the like of them no man can
Easily find in a long summer's day.

A different experiment is seen in "The Howling Song
of Al-Mohara." Here the rhyme scheme of the eighteen-
line stanzas achieves subtle and appropriate effects. The
last stanza reads:

> Can Sultans, can the Guilty Rich
>   Purchase with mines and thrones a draught,
>   Allah, Allah hu!
> From that Nutulian fount of which
>   The Conscience-tortured whilome quaffed
>   Allah, Allah hu!
> Vain dream! Power, Glory, Riches, Craft,
> Prove magnets for the Sword of Wrath;
>   Allah, Allah hu!
> Thornplant Man's last and lampless path,
>   And barb the Slaying Angel's shaft;
>   Allah, Allah hu!
>   O' the Bloodguilty ever sees
>   But sights that make him rue,
> As I do now, and cry therefore,
> All night long, on my knees,
>   Evermore,
>   Allah, Allah hu!

The first sestet sets a clear pattern: *abcabc*. But the
reversals in the second sestet slow down the motion and
make the middle lines the strongest unit. The final
sestet, with another kind of reversal, receives less emphasis because it serves almost as a refrain, in which
the same three rhymes are repeated in each stanza.

The tone of the Oriental poems is most often melan-
cholic, but despite the familiar gloom there is often

a playful manner found here that Mangan discards in his Irish poems and original poems. For instance in "Advice (From the Ottoman)," each stanza closes with an anagram of the opening word, such as "emit"/ "Time," "room"/"Moore," and "live"/"Evil." His anti-English satire is heavy-handed but still amusing in the poem "To the Ingleeze Khafir Calling Himself Djaun Bool Djenkinzun." The English colonial's funny physical appearance and still odder clothing are mocked by a Persian native. O'Donoghue's suggestion that the attribution which serves as a subtitle, "Thus Writeth Meer Djafrit," means "mere chaff writ" seems plausible, and this is certainly Mangan's own joke, rather than any seventeenth-century Persian poet's.

* * *

From Spanish and Italian and other languages he published scores of translations, some of which have real merit. But the group of translations for which he is best remembered are his poems from the Irish. These were the products of the last decade of his life, and primarily of the last few years. Although he is reported to have known some Irish, Mangan did not translate these poems directly; for the most part, they are based on prose translations done by Eugene O'Curry, although the sources of a few poems have been ascertained to be John O'Donovan and Samuel Ferguson. In 1849, shortly after Mangan's death, these translations were collected by John O'Daly, and published in *The Poets and Poetry of Munster*.

Like the German poems, these pieces are usually not scrupulously faithful translations; some range so far from the originals that they should be read as Mangan's own. But many of them express perfectly the tone and sentiment of the Irish versions, even when the exact words do not correspond. And, most important, they feature a dazzling array of experiments in technique and structure. Patrick Power estimates that in half of the Irish translations in O'Donoghue's edition, Mangan uses the original Irish meters, although none of them are the authentic, strict bardic meter. Nevertheless, he comes close to the old measure, the rules of which are lengthy and detailed, but include requiring seven syllables in each line, with two or more accented syllables, set end and internal rhymes and a shifted accent at the end of alternate lines. Mangan's practice is to set up some dominant rhythm, often sustained by uneven lines, and employ strong rhymes, alliteration and assonance. And the variety of effects achieved is impressive. So successful is his handling of the new measures that Padraic Colum has written, "To the Irish poet who must write in English he has given a form that is distinctly Gaelic."

The best of his poems from the Irish, and the single poem by which he is most widely remembered, is "Dark Rosaleen." It is based on Samuel Ferguson's version of a seventeenth-century poem by the poet Costello of Ballyhaunis, County Mayo. Mangan published several versions of the poem under the title "Roisin Dubh," the original Irish title, but this is the most free and the best of his translations of it. It is, of course, a patriotic poem, addressed to Ireland, speaking hope for her future, if only through warfare. And for all its exclamations and familiar metaphors, it is a stirring poem, whose power results from its remarkably strong cadence and brave sentiments. Yet there is subtle artistic craft beneath the surface. The poem's seven stanzas sustain the allegory of Ireland as the loved one, a scheme probably necessary at the time of the original poem's composition: during the insurrections by the northern clans, such appeals could be labelled as treasonous. As on other occasions in Ireland's history aid from Rome and Spain were expected but "wine from the royal Pope" and "Spanish ale" never arrived.

The poem opens with an exhortation to Ireland to be brave and wait for help. The poet is inspired, enflamed by his love, and in the third stanza addresses her as "my queen, my life of life, my saint of saints." The next three stanzas develop those images: Ireland is a dethroned queen, who will soon reign again alone; she will bring success to the poet's efforts through prayer and give him "a second life, a soul anew." So inspired is his quest that success is assured, and even the violence foretold in the last stanza will not be in vain, for Ireland will not die until the Judgment Day.

The verse techniques reveal further complexities: The opening couplet of each stanza is in anapestic verse, while the rest of the stanza reverts to iambic lines, alternating tetrameter and trimeter, for the most part. But the rhyme scheme reveals a different stanzaic structure, divided into three parts: a quatrain rhyming *abab*, and two quatrains rhyming *caca* and *acca*. Thus, the rhymed couplet, lines 10 and 11, form a single strong statement before the final refrain. But there are other complications yet: the refrain, "My dark Rosaleen," is a much shorter line, repeated three times in each stanza, with slight variations. In each stanza but one there is ellipsis in the fifth line, causing a stronger pause; in the last stanza, the most assertive one, this caesura is omitted. The final stanza of this poem well reveals the artistry of the whole:

> O! the Erne shall run red
>   With redundance of blood,
> The earth shall rock beneath our tread,
>   And flames wrap hill and wood,
> And gun-peal, and slogan cry,
>   Wake many a glen serene,
> Ere you shall fade, ere you shall die,
>   My Dark Rosaleen!
>   My own Rosaleen!
> The Judgment Hour must first be nigh,
> Ere you can fade, ere you can die,
>   My Dark Rosaleen!

"Owen Reilly: A Keen" is a simpler and more tender poem. It is spoken by a mother on the death of her son. But here, as in the previous poem, the unusual metrical and stanzaic forms clearly set a tone and build to emphasis. Its first stanza goes:

> Oh! lay aside the flax, and put away the wheel,
>   And sing with me, but not in gladness—
> The heart that's in my breast is like to break with sadness—
>   God, God alone knows what I feel!

The same rhyme scheme is sustained throughout its sixteen stanzas. In each, the middle couplet is a feminine rhyme, ending on a weak syllable. But although the second and fourth lines are both short, the last line is consistently one syllable shorter, slightly out of rhythm, and much more powerful: "God, God alone knows what I feel."

"Lament for Banba," based on the Irish of Aodhagán O'Rathaille, is also composed of uneven lines of ana-pestic verse, following a regular rhyme scheme, except for the refrain, "Alas, alas, and alas!/ For the once proud people of Banba!" That refrain does not fit into the rhyme scheme, and in its irregularity of meter and rhyme, seems all the more forceful and striking.

"Ellen Bawn" and "The Woman of Three Cows" both employ the long line characteristic of some early Irish poetry. In the latter poem, the strong rhythm re-quired to sustain such a long line and the feminine rhymes fit the playful mockery of the subject: the pre-tentious woman, proud because she has so little more than her neighbors. But "Ellen Bawn" is a love poem, filled with hyperbole and expressions of ardor. Here the strong rhythm distracts from the subject, particularly in the last stanza, where macabre imagery reminiscent of the poetry of Synge concludes the poem:

Would to God that in the sod my corpse to-night were lying,
And the wild birds wheeling o'er it, and the winds a-sighing,
Since your cruel mother and your kindred choose to sever
Two hearts that Love would blend in one for ever and for
    ever!

"O'Hussey's Ode to the Maguire" also has a long line, but it is not so regular or musical as these other poems. For that reason, the poem is far more effective. Another instance of the Gaelic long line is Mangan's version of "Kathaleen Ny-Houlahan," the personification of Ireland. James Joyce, in his 1902 essay on Mangan, praised this poem for its masterful variation from trochaic to "firm, marching iambs." Equally impressive are the poet's uses of internal rhyme, alliteration and assonance, as revealed in the closing stanza:

He, who over sands and waves led Israel along—
He, who fed, with heavenly bread, that chosen tribe throng—
He, who stood by Moses, when his foes were fierce and
    strong—
May He show forth His might in saving Kathaleen Ny-
    Houlahan.

Long as these lines are, the parallel structures of the first three lines accumulate rhetorical force so that the final line proceeds without an internal pause and with real majesty.

"The Dawning of the Day," on the other hand, is written in very short, roughly anapestic lines, with a set rhyme scheme. But the dominant rhythm and frequent stops fit the kaleidescopic progress of scenes, from an idyllic county setting to a battle, then to heaven and finally to the end of the dream. In a footnote, Mangan attributes political implications to the poet, O'Doran, but these are, in fact, very slight in the original. As in "Dark Rosaleen," help from abroad is hoped for, but the poem's only comment is an ironic one: it was all a dream. The poem's conclusion embodies some cynicism:

> Cities girt with glorious gardens,
> (Whose immortal
> Habitants, in robes of light,
> Stood, methought, as angel-wardens

Nigh each portal,)
Now arose to daze my sight.
Eden spread around, revived and blooming;
When . . . lo! as I gazed, all passed away.
I saw but black rocks and billows blooming
In the dim chill dawn of day.

Although his translations are not scholarly or literal, Mangan did succeed in conveying the spirit of classic Irish poems and even a sense of their structures. Roibeard O'Faracháin calls him "the best *poet* who had so far translated. . . . He came, perhaps, a little nearer than anyone before him to reproduction of the formal elements of his originals, though he never attempted completeness of this kind."

The best method of assessing Mangan's skills as a translator is to compare his versions with those of others. Here is a representative stanza of "O'Hussey's Ode to the Maguire" as Mangan presents it:

An awful, a tremendous night is this, meseems!
The flood-gates of the rivers of heaven, I think, have been burst wide—
Down from the overcharged clouds, like unto headlong ocean's tide,
Descends grey rain in roaring streams.

The original Irish reads as follows:

> Do h-osgladh as ochtuibh neóil
> Doirse uisgidhe an aidheóir,
> Tug sé minlinnte ann a muir,
> Do sgeith an firmimint a hurbhuidh.

Douglas Hyde's literal translation of that is:

There has been thrown open, out of the bosom of the clouds, the doors of the waters of the air. It has made of little linns a sea; the firmament has belched forth her destructiveness.

And a recent translation of the same passage by Frank O'Connor reads:

> The floodgates of the heavens yawn
> Above the bosom of the clouds;
>   And every pool a sea,
>   And murder in the air.

As can be seen, neither Mangan nor O'Connor attempted to reproduce the complex internal rhymes of *Deibhidh* meter, in which the original is written. But Mangan's use of regular rhythms and rhymes is as appropriate to the subject as O'Connor's briefer unrhymed rendition. Here, as in some other poems, it is clear that Mangan is padding in order to sustain a stronger rhythm, but his amplification does achieve a cadence expressive of the grief of the poet.

A similar practice is seen in the comparison of Mangan's version of Geoffrey Keating's "The Sorrows of Innisfail" with that of Padraic Pearse, entitled "From My Grief on Fal's Proud Plain." First Mangan's verse:

Oh! lived the Princes of Ainy's plains, and the heroes of
  green Domgole,
And the chiefs of the Maigue, we still might hope to baffle
  our doom and dole,
Well then might the dastards shiver who herd by the blue
  Bride river,
    But ah! those great and glorious men
    Shall draw no glaive on Earth again!

Pearse's poem includes the following:

If the high chief lived of Aine and Druim Draoile
And the strong lions of Maigue who granted gifts

There surely were no place for this rabble where
  Bride meets Blackwater,
But shouts and outcries on high announcing their ruin
  and rout.

The second is too obviously a translation, in which
the odd figures of speech do not come naturally; Mangan's poem, for all its artifice and conscious poetic
tricks, does not show the strain of transferring an idea
from another language. It can stand as a poem on its
own.

Mangan's translation of "Prince Alfrid's Itinerary
Through Ireland" is very close to the original in word-
ing and tone, although the rhymes are sometimes forced
and the rhythm very strong. The same criticism is properly made of "Cean-Salla," where the strain to find a
rhyme word for the title forces him to use such teeth-
gritting line ends as "enthral a" and "I fall a."

But some of the very excesses of Mangan's renditions
—the multiple rhymes both within lines and in double
and triple end rhymes—are, paradoxically, the most
authentic Irish elements. Nevertheless, the strong rhythm characteristic of all of Mangan's verse does at times
become dominant. In poems on other than humorous
or heroic subjects, this is unlikely to happen, but in
poems of melancholy or love, anapestic and other toe-
tapping measures do detract from the meaning of the
poems.

At his best, Mangan succeeds in combining pleasing
musical effects with surprising but functional metrical
and stanzaic forms. Although it is not a translation but
a paraphrase from Scripture, "Lamentation of Jeremias

Over Jerusalem" serves well at this point to indicate the effects possible. The first stanza reads:

> How doth she sit alone,
> The city late so thronged; how doth she sit in woe,
> Begirt with solitude and graves!
> Oh! how is she that from her Temple-throne
> Ruled o'er the Gentiles, now become
> A widow in her dreary home!
> How have her Princes fallen low,
> And dwindled into slaves!

The rhythm is iambic and the lines are of uneven length, but a set stanzaic form is maintained, in which a rhymed couplet interrupts the symmetrical arrangement of two triplets (*abcaddbc*). The subject he adopted from the Lamentations is, of course, a compatible one for Mangan, whose original verse often treats similar subjects of near despair and regret over the ruins of the world.

III

Mangan's original poems have received less critical attention than his translations, but a number of them deserve careful reevaluation. Like the translations, they are often experimental in technique, and employ a wide range of metrical and stanzaic schemes. In subject matter, they range from humorous extravaganzas to religious and patriotic verse.

Mangan's earliest published poem is "Genius," which he included in the portion of his *Autobiography* that has survived. It is most fascinating as it reveals the talents and attitudes of the poet at age sixteen. Already he saw himself as burdened by his exceptional gifts. He recognized that not all his suffering was imposed by others who misunderstood his sensitive nature; his sorrows, he saw, resulted primarily from his inner "unshared shroudedness of lot." The verse form of the poem is rhymed iambic pentameter and the rhyme scheme is simple and functional, marking off the major divisions of the poem. The first eight lines form one unit, sustained by a clear rhyme scheme. The next ten lines begin with the same end rhyme and form a second distinct unit. There follows a four-line transitional section with alternating lines of rhyme. And the poem closes with a seven-line section composed of facing rhymed triplets, followed by a strong, final alexandrine. In its total effect, it is a highly polished, clear and forceful poem, particularly when considered as an instance of Mangan's juvenalia.

"The Nameless One," composed in 1842 or thereabouts, is also autobiographical and treats the sufferings of his childhood and his present state. But despite the enormous popularity of this poem, second in that respect only to "Dark Rosaleen," it now seems self-pitying and morbid. His assessment of his own poetry is accurate, at least in describing the bulk of his composition; he calls it "perchance not deep, but intense and rapid." And as a biographical source the poem does convey the horror with which Mangan viewed life and the longing he felt for death.

The taste for the morbid seen in that poem seems to have begun early. In "Lines, Written at Seventeen," which is not included in O'Donoghue's edition of the poetry, Mangan dwells on death in a grim way:

> The sun's rich rays have often thrown
> A gleam upon the lonely tomb,
> And all without hath brightly shone
> While all within was ghastly gloom.
>
> * * *
>
> Thus may a transient smile impart
> Its radiance to the care-worn cheek
> While all within the tomb-like heart
> Is dark and drear and coldly bleak.

Some of the gloom may be attributed to the cynicism of the very young. But the subject occurs often; "Rest

Only in the Grave" concludes that neither wealth nor love nor any activity can provide the peace for which he is seeking. Only death can grant it.

This morbid strain is seen in a number of his other original poems. "The Dying Enthusiast" expresses the poet's longing for "Prison-bursting death." But the tone of this poem is assertive and the strong rhythm set by opening each line on a stressed syllable does not seem inappropriate. Again, the rhyme of lines of uneven length serves to divide the poem into units, with each stanza leading up to the cry, "Oh! no! no!" for its final line. "The One Mystery" also bewails man's state:

> No more, no more—with aching brow
> And restless heart, and burning brain,
> We ask the When, the Where, the How,
> And ask in vain.

But the language is unoriginal and the sentiment seems shallow.

In "A Broken-Hearted Lay" Mangan expresses his rejection of "the inanity of all things human," and specifies the two things which most plague him in his life: "the dark ingratitude of man" and "the hollower perfidy of woman." He concludes that all that awaits him in his future life are pain, bitterness, "torturing thoughts that will not be forbidden,/ And agonies that cannot all be hidden!" In the poem written on the death of Catherine Hayes, a young girl he had once taught, he sees death as a deliverance and "this blank world a prison and a grave." Therefore, he cannot regret that she escaped while life still seemed a joy. The concluding stanza of "Life is the Desert and the Solitude" serves as a summary of this common theme in Mangan's verse:

> Alas! for those who stand alone—
>   The shrouded few who feel and know
> What none beside have felt and known
>   To all of such a mould below
> Is born an undeparting woe,
>   Beheld by none and shared with none—
> A cankering worm whose work is slow,
>   But gnaws the heart-strings one by one,
> And drains the bosom's blood till the last
>   drop be gone.

Despite the impressive effect achieved by using a much longer line to close each stanza, the diction and sentiments of this poem are unconvincing. Mangan is seen here in his weakest position, and the grief, which was no doubt sincere, and the impression of futility, which is undeniably felt, become shrill and whining when repeated in so many poems.

However, all of the poems quoted on this subject are the products of the 1830s or earlier. In the last ten years of his life, Mangan became more positive, although not optimistic, in his poetry. If he never changed his view of life as an extended torture, he saw his role as a more active one: that of seer or prophet, particularly of Ireland's destiny.

Ireland had been the subject of some of his early poetry also. "To My Native Land" appeared in 1832, but it carries no strong conviction, relying as it does on stock images of harps and empty halls. From the 1840s, when he became involved with the Young Ireland group, even though his association was never a close one, his verse becomes more convincingly patriotic and more assertive in other ways as well.

The heritage of the New Critics and twentieth-century literary criticism in general equips us well for the analysis of personal lyrics, especially of an ironic sort, where language and imagery can be weighed for delicate and often ambiguous effects. We even feel well qualified in the analysis of narrative poems, where characters and plot structure can be analyzed in almost the same ways we approach drama. But public poetry, in which rhetorical techniques are used to move or convince a wide audience, and in which subtlety is not a necessary virtue—this large and respectable body of poetry evades our modern approaches. The problem is apparent in the later poetry of Mangan's contemporary, Alfred Lord Tennyson. The genuine power of his patriotic poems is not usually denied, but the obvious subjects and obtrusive sentiments of "The Charge of the Light Brigade" or "Ode on the Death of the Duke of Wellington" do not attract our literary critics. And yet, the proven and lasting appeal of Tennyson's public poems, and Kipling's as well, should make us find the method and the terms by which to analyse them. Undeniably Mangan's patriotic poems, like those of these English poets, lack internal subtlety. But since their intention is to bestir a wide audience to confidence in their nation or to remind them of Ireland's sorrows, subtlety may be sacrificed to other effects. With these public poems, more than the personal lyrics, a rhetorical approach, proceeding from identifying the effects of the poems on the reader to analyzing the techniques employed would seem most useful. The techniques range from choice of words to figures of speech, to use of ethical and emotional appeals and even poetic forms. No more than with other literary works can the poet's exact intentions here be ascertained, and we must concentrate on the relation of the poem to its readers.

The continued appeal of Mangan's patriotic poems cannot be denied. "Dark Rosaleen" and "The Warning Voice," when recited with unashamed gusto, can still send shivers up the spine of even the most apolitical man of the 1970s. Rudi Holzapfel, one of the most talented of the young poets writing in Ireland today, and himself a highly respected Mangan scholar, calls Mangan Ireland's greatest poet, barring none. Clearly it is his patriotic appeal which Holzapfel has in mind when he writes:[1]

> Mangan is a dangerous hero. If you like Synge you can always go to the Aran Islands and curse Manhattan to the roar of the Western Sea; if you like Joyce you get drunk in his Martello Tower and spew it all out at Forty Foot. If you like Yeats you can sit in the shadow of Ben Bulben and read A. Norman Jeffares. But if you like Mangan you start to weep the wrongs and woes of Erin, and you reach for your pike. That is the difference. It is one hell of a difference.

It is not surprising that Mangan took up the subject of Ireland's sorrows. It would be more remarkable if an Irishman, no matter how alienated from human society, could ignore the horrors of the late 1840s, when famine and several waves of cholera epidemics racked the coun-

---

1. Rudi Holzapfel, "Dangerous Hero" *Hibernia* XXXII (November 1, 1968), p. 11.

try. Between 1845 and 1851 approximately a million died and about another million emigrated, so that the population of Ireland was reduced by one-fourth in that short span of time. Those who survived did so only after severe suffering. In the single year 1849 almost one million Irishmen were kept in a workhouse for some period.

"The Warning Voice," one of Mangan's best patriotic poems, was written in 1846, at the start of this bleak period. The pervading rhythm of the poem is anapestic; rhyme is frequent and up to the last stanza the lines are usually only two stresses in length. But the emphasis on fewer words in each line allows the poem to grow in intensity. Textbook descriptions of various metrical effects claim that anapestic verse has the effect of being light and lilting. But the final six lines of this poem show how strong and majestic it can be:

> So, howe'er, as frail men, you have erred
> Your way along Life's thronged road,
> Shall your consciences prove a sure guerdon
> And tower of defence,
> Until Destiny summon you hence
> To the Better Abode!

Leading up to this conclusion, the poem speaks to the people of Ireland, recognizing their causes for sorrow and foreseeing even further hazards ahead, until in the next generation some peace may reign.

The moving effect on modern readers is due to a number of rhetorical techniques and devices, such as the use of direct address, repeated parallel structures

and personification. The poem opens with an appeal
to the reader:

> Ye Faithful—ye noble!
> A day is at hand
> Of trial and trouble,
> And woe in the land!

The parallelism of the first line is echoed in the alliteration of the third. The rhyme is strong: the last accented
syllable always has a rhyme within the stanza. But the
stanzas progress in length, so that the last of the five
stanzas is almost four times as long as the first. By this,
as well as by the parallel structures of so many statements, a climax is built up to in the last stanza, which
sets forth the message of following the course of virtue.
The message is neither explicit nor detailed; a clear
course of action is not prescribed; but the cadence of
the verse is so strong and the diction is so elevated that
its effect is strong nevertheless.

"A Voice of Encouragement—A New Year's Lay"
appeared in *The Nation* on January 1, 1848, in the
middle of the Famine. The verse form is unusual:
primarily dactylic measure with six stresses in each
line, an unusually long line. Mangan's awareness of the
horror of the Famine is painful to the reader:

> Friends! the gloom in our land, in our once bright land
>   grows deeper.
> Suffering, even to death, in its horriblest forms, aboundeth;
> Thro' our black harvestless fields, the peasants' faint wail
>   resoundeth.
> Hark to it, even now! . . . The nightmare oppressed sleeper
> Gasping and struggling for life, beneath his hideous be-
>   strider,

Seeth not, dreeth not, sight or terror more fearful or ghastly
Than that poor paralysed slave! Want, Houselessness, Famine, and lastly
Death in a thousand-corpsed grave, that momently waxeth
   wider.

But worse than that, in terms of the future, is the
irresponsibility of Ireland's leaders, who have despaired
and surrendered their ideals. Nevertheless, Mangan
counsels hope and activity. The Carlylean advice of
working and fulfilling one's duty reminds us of Mangan's very Victorian attitudes. Like Carlyle and his
English contemporaries, Mangan sees himself as a poet-
prophet. Once again, the conclusion is not any clearly
stated solution. Images of the coming millenium are
given, to be heralded by "The Envoy":

Cloaked in the Hall, the Envoy stands, his mission unspoken,
While the pale, banquetless guests await in trembling to
   hear it.

The atmosphere of confusion and suffering which
precedes the coming reign of peace and justice pre-
figures Yeats's poems of his middle period. The scenes
described in such poems as "Easter 1916" and "The
Second Coming" are not far in tone from those described by Mangan:

Slavery debased the soul; yea! reverses its primal nature;
Long were our fathers bowed to the earth with fetters of
   iron—
And, alas! we inherit the failings and ills that environ
Slaves like a dungeon wall and dwarf their original stature.
Look on your countrymen's failings with less of anger than
   pity;
Even with the faults of the evil deal in a manner half tender;

And like an army encamped before a beleaguered city,
Earlier or later you must compel your foes to surrender!

   Although his political message is not made specific
in these poems, Mangan had allied himself with the
Young Ireland movement by this time. But by 1849,
the group was disbanded and its efforts toward a revolution had failed. Mangan seems disheartened but not
yet hopeless in "Soul and Country," which was published during the last year of his life. The previous year
of revolutions on the continent gave signs that "a
struggling world would yet be free/ And live anew."
But so far it had not been accomplished, and, in Ireland,
prospects were more dim than ever before. The second
stanza reads:

>   Look round, my soul, and see and say
>   If those about thee understand
>   Their mission here;
>   The will to smite—the power to slay—
>   Abound in every heart and hand,
>   Afar, anear.
>   But, God! must yet the conqueror's sword
>   Pierce *mind*, as heart, in this proud year?
>   O, dream it not!
>   It sounds a false, blaspheming word,
>   Begot and born of mortal fear—
>   And ill-begot.

Much of the power of this stanza, and the entire poem,
results from the air of desperation and confusion. Bitter
rhetorical questions are asked and answers are attempted. Even the last statement, in which "begot" is
repeated, with an ironic twist, well fits the mood of
resentment. By now, no political formulae can be found
that can solve the immense problems; in the last stanza

of the poem, Mangan turns to religious faith as the only possible source of help. But the conclusion is staggering in its force:

> Beseech your God, and bide your hour—
> He cannot, will not, long be dumb;
> Even now His tread
> Is heard o'er earth with coming power;
> And coming, trust me, it will come,
> Else were He dead!

The force of the last line, with all its desperation, is accumulated partly by its irregular meter. This is probably the strongest, most moving of Mangan's poetic statements.

"A Vision of Connaught in the Thirteenth Century" was written several years earlier, and illustrates a more fanciful side of even his political verse. It describes a dream vision which reminds us of Coleridge's "Kubla Khan" in its odd imagery:

> Then saw I thrones,
> And circling fires,
> And a Dome rose near me, as by a spell,
> Whence flowed the tones
> Of silver lyres,
> And many voices in wreathed swell;
> And their thrilling chime
> Fell on mine ears
> As the heavenly hymn of an angel-band—
> "It is now the time,
> These be the years,
> Of Cáhal Mór of the Wine-red Hand!"

The lines are written in accentual verse with two and four stresses in each line, and the rhyme scheme is simple and functional. But the poem is too short; hardly is the scene described, and some premonitions

of impending defeat given, when the speaker ends his
dream and the poem concludes.

A completely different kind of poem is "Gasparo
Bandollo," which is a narrative poem set in Italy. In
the *Autobiography* Mangan indicated that his own
father had much in common with the title character
of this poem. In it, a fugitive Italian patriot, Sevrini,
is betrayed by Giambattista, the son of the title character. When the father learns of his son's act, he dis-
owns him and shoots him, while the son kneels before
him begging for mercy. At the end, the focus is on
Gasparo, who is left suffering and hopeless, not because
he did the wrong thing, but because there seems to be
nothing left for which to live. The situation reminds
us of Matthew Arnold's "Sohrab and Rustum" and,
as in that poem, images of water symbolize man's destiny. The poem ends:

> Onwards in power the wide flood rolls
> Whose thunder-waves wake evermore
> The caverned soul of each far shore,
> But when the midnight storm-wind sweeps
> In wrath about its broken deeps,
> What heart but ponders darkly over
> The myriad wrecks those waters cover!
> It is the lonely brook alone
> That winds its way with Music's tone
>   By orange bower and lily-blossom,
> And sinks into the Parent Wave,
> Not as worn Age into its grave,
>   But as pure Childhood on God's bosom.

This is a late poem, written in the last few years of
his life; it is more restrained in its use of rhyme and
rhythm. The relevance of the Italian uprising to Ire-

land's politics in the late 1840s is evident enough, but it is not belabored in any way. Rather the theme shifts from political concerns to personal loss, and finally to the consolation of religious faith.

Mangan's life was short, and at his death his poetry was at a point of great promise. He wrote a good deal—too much perhaps—and shows remarkable versatility both in subject matter and technique. Experiments in practically every metrical and stanzaic form abound in his work, and the devices of rhetoric as well as of versification are employed in a startling variety of manners. Although his poems of patriotism and his translations have been stressed in this survey, his religious poetry and humorous verse also deserve rereading. Of the latter category, "A Fast Keeper" is representative. It plays on a single pun of "Lent," and complains of his loss of some money loaned to his friend Bentley. One other, "The Metempsychosis," based on a poem by Ignaz Castelli, holds a natural fascination for any reader of Joyce's *Ulysses*. But it is also a pure *tour de force*, playing with rhyme in a manner matched only by Ogden Nash:

To go on with my catalogue: what will you bet I've seen a
Goose, that was reckoned in her day a pretty-faced young
    woman?
But more than that, I knew at once a bloody-lipped hyena
To've been a Russian Marshal, or an ancient Emperor
    (Roman)
All snakes and vipers, toads and reptiles, crocodiles and
    crawlers
I set down as court sycophants or hypocritic bawlers,
And there I may've been right or wrong—but nothing can
    be truer
Than this, that in a scorpion I beheld a vile reviewer.

"To Joseph Brenan" is one of Mangan's final compositions. It was written within a month of his death, in reply to that poet's tribute to Mangan, published in *The Irishman*. In Brenan's poem Mangan is praised for his delicate use of sound, and for its embodiment of meaning. He is likened to Prospero and to Swedenborg, and is praised in particular as a scholar of German literature. In Mangan's reply, Brenan is compared briefly with Shelley, but then the poem turns to Mangan's defense of his own life. He agrees that he has worked hard at his poetry, despite his own weaknesses. Often he has been close to despair, but he was rescued by his faith. In imagery similar to that of Francis Thompson's "The Hound of Heaven," God is portrayed as tracking him down and saving him from total defeat. For himself, he sees a clear duty: "to live a bard, in thought and feeling . . . to act my rhyme, by self-restraint."

IV

In 1904, D. J. O'Donoghue, Mangan's biographer and the editor of the most comprehensive edition of his poems, published a collection of a dozen of his prose pieces. In his introduction to the volume, O'Donoghue is modest in his claims for the prose: "The reader will hardly expect to find anything so distinguished as in the Poems—the magical power which enabled Mangan to rise from height to height of poetical achievement is almost altogether absent." Admittedly, the strong political themes that inspire his best original poetry do not appear in his prose. And it is true that the author's verbal facility is less exercised in the prose than in his best poems. But the prose writings do exhibit their author's broad interests and love of word play, as well as his bizarre sense of humor. So entertaining, in fact, are some of the prose pieces that they do not deserve to be filed away only in an edition so long out of print.

Two of the prose works in O'Donoghue's edition are short stories reminiscent of stories by Gothic novelists, like Charles Maturin or Edgar Allan Poe. They treat the same central subjects that appear in so much of Mangans' work: the alienated man, damned to wander alone

61

because of some demonic curse; the unhappy love affair; and the desperation of a man under heavy debts.

"The Thirty Flasks" centers on a young man, Basil Von Rosenwald, who has lost all his valuables and accumulated huge debts at gambling. To pay off what he owes, Basil is directed by a friend to a mysterious rich man of untold wealth and unknown background. An air of mystery is set as the friend admits that he has sent two others to the man before: one is dead and another has entered a monastery. But Basil does go to the Nabob, despite some misgivings. When he arrives at the house, Basil is shocked by the man's grotesque appearance: he is dwarfish, deformed, hardly human. The Nabob claims to be Basil's own brother who he had understood was dead; but the Nabob tells a story of being kidnapped and sold as a slave. Eventually, he claims, he got to India and spent ten years there studying magic.

Without hesitation, the Nabob offers to give Basil one thousand ducats, providing that for such amount, he will drink a flask of some mysterious and magical potion, the Black Elixir. The result is predicted: each flask he drinks will transfer one inch of his height to the Nabob, who, at three and a half feet, wants to grow to Basil's six foot height. In order to keep off his creditors and to gain the hand of Aurelia Von Elsberg, his beloved, Basil does drink one flask, and suffers what seem to be only momentary effects. After drinking a second flask the next day, he goes into a trance, described as much like an opium dream. But soon the threatened effects become evident: Basil realizes that he is losing inches steadily.

Before he completely loses his identity, that is, after he has taken twenty-nine flasks, Basil discovers that the Nabob is really the Oriental magician Maugraby. At almost the last moment, Basil is saved: he learns from a stranger that he has inherited a huge fortune. The stranger goes with him to see Maugraby, and once there confronts the magician with what he knows. On being discovered, the Nabob uses magic to escape: he blows up house and all, but when the dust settles, Basil is again six feet tall. All ends happily, with Basil and Aurelia married, and the magician still plying his tricks in Alexandria.

However silly the story line is, the plot moves quickly and suspense is well maintained right to the end. But Mangan cannot resist verbal play, even when it detracts from the tone of the story. The money lender dunning Basil is named Herr Grabb and the stranger who confronts Maugraby is called Rubbadub Snook-snacker Slickwitz. The narrative moves along with regular asides and humorous turns:

> He got up and dressed himself and shaved—or shaved and dressed himself, we forget which—and then he actually breakfasted; and if the curious in dietetics are agog to know of what his breakfast consisted we will gratify them:—it consisted of one colossal roll and butter, two hen eggs, three slices of Westphalia ham, and four cups of Arabian coffee—a breakfast we undertake to recommend to themselves, the curious aforesaid. After he had finished his last cup, it is a fact that he drew his chair to the fire and deposited his toes on the fender; and, settled in that position, began to pick his teeth and think of Aurelia.

More serious and more remarkable for its biographical relevance is the story entitled "The Man in the Cloak." Mangan himself used that appellation as the author of "My Bugle and How I Blow It," and in that essay analyzed the implications of each important word in the phrase. Autobiographical associations occur in this story also, although they are oblique.

The story opens with a scene of Johann Klaus Braunbrock, a bank cashier, forging a draft as part of his embezzlement plan. He is interrupted by a stranger who demands that a check in his name be cashed; he signs the check merely "M.—The Man in the Cloak." As the plot proceeds, the title character reappears several times; each time he reveals that he knows more about the crime Braunbrock is committing. His identity is never revealed, except for his initial, "M," and the fact that he is an Irishman. He indicates that he knows all and can do anything, but, he says, "I cannot conquer my own destiny." Frequent allusions to the devil and demons are made, and his damned state becomes evident.

Once he has stolen the money, Braunbrock has planned to elope with the woman he loves, Livonia. But when he visits her it is revealed that she loves someone else and feels only contempt for the bank clerk. He takes her to the theatre, where the Man in the Cloak again confronts him, and accuses him of forgery. To show what lies ahead, the stranger magically portrays Braunbrock's crime on the stage; there, after stealing the money, Braunbrock is shown apprehended and imprisoned. It is all a vision created by the mysterious stranger, but it has the intended effect: Braunbrock makes some sort of a secret pact with the Man in the

Cloak. Immediately, police arrive, arrest the stranger for Braunbrock's crimes, and take him away. However, when they arrive at the police station, the body they had tied up and taken has become only a scarecrow made of a pile of straw, rags, and a pumpkin.

As a result of the secret agreement, Braunbrock himself becomes the Man in the Cloak. He turns on Livonia, discovers her lover in a closet, and predicts that man's capture for his recent treasonous activities. He is vicious in denouncing the faithless, deceiving woman he had loved. But left alone, Braunbrock is seen to have inherited nearly limitless powers and wealth. Predictably, all pleasure soon palls as he becomes more aware of his damned state.

Like his predecessor, he must find a victim who will release him from the curse and take it on himself. One night he has a dream about the man from whom he inherited his title and his doom; he sees him in the Church of St. Sulpice at Paris. He leaves immediately for that place, but when he arrives he finds that the man he is looking for is now dead; a priest tells him that the man's name was . . . Melmoth. After wandering through his miserable life, that man had died penitent and forgiven.

The priest convinces Braunbrock also to pray, which he does, and feels great relief. But the curse is not lifted until he meets Malaventure, a Persian, who agrees to sell his soul, and take on the curse. After this, the talisman of the curse changes hands several times and, it is reported, its progress may have stopped in one man's suicide in the Seine.

That Mangan associated the cursed wanderer with

himself is apparent from his descriptions and the force
with which he describes that doomed state:

> The enormous nature of his power only made him ac-
> quainted with the essential desolation of heart which
> flows from being alone in the universe and unsympathized
> with by others. The relations that had existed between
> his finer faculties and the external world gradually suf-
> fered an awful and indescribable change. Like his pre-
> decessor, he could in an instant transport himself into the
> blooming valleys of the East, or the swarthy deserts of
> Africa; the treasures of the earth were his, and the ocean
> bared her deeps, teeming with gold and lustrous jewels,
> before him. But the transitions and vicissitudes by which
> mortals are taught to appreciate pain and pleasure, and
> the current of life is guaranteed from stagnating, were
> lost to him.

As in the previous story, however, Mangan cannot
resist puns, and succumbs to one even at one of the
most dramatic moments in the story. Braunbrock is
challenged to a duel by Livonia's lover:

> "Draw this instant, I say!"
> "You would have better success in calling on me for
> a song; though we are in a drawing room . . . I have
> never learned to draw, though singing and dancing are
> very much in my way,—favorite amusements of mine."

Most remarkable about this story is the real artistry
of the narrative technique. The story opens with a scene
of activity diminishing and narrowing to the scene of
Braunbrock alone in his "temporary prison," nervously
perpetrating the forgery. Throughout the tale only the
scenes of most striking action are presented, while much
is left unsaid. The central issue of the diabolic contract
is not fully revealed until the end of the story, and even

then there are details which mystify, such as the final passage. After finishing the story, Mangan adds a newspaper account of an astrologer inquiring about the suicide which ended the main plot. This eccentric German attempts to analyse the action in terms of astrology and the mystical theories of Jakob Boehme, the sixteenth-century German philosopher. However, his interpretations are only laughed at, and he leaves. Rather than merely being appended to the story, the astrological reference seems to add a comment on the whole mystery, since the German remarks on Jupiter being an arch-demon, and somehow determining what has occurred. All elements of the story: the fantastic, the mysterious, the autobiographical and the humorous aspects blend to form a single memorable work.

In forms other than short stories, Mangan wrote on a wide variety of subjects. His affinities to German writers of his day are evident in his essay, "Chapters on Ghostcraft," in which he discusses the issues arising from Justinus Kerner's books on the Ghost Seeress of Prevorst and similar books on the Supernatural. However sincerely Mangan was interested in the subject, his treatment of it in this essay is playful and ironic. He comments on the spreading refutation of non-belief in ghosts, "incredulism," and quotes extensively from the amazing or amusing ghost stories recounted by "Madame Hauffer, High Priestess of Mysticism." In his playful manner, as well as in the sincerity of some parts of the essay, Mangan here reminds us of Carlyle in *Sartor Resartus*. Like Carlyle's editor, the narrator of this essay addresses his audience as "spectacled reader," talks to him as an equal about a variety of the most esoteric subjects, and yet speaks with a moralizing, almost evangelistic fervor about following certain ethical rules. A paragraph from the conclusion illustrates some of these parallels:

> Perpend and ponder this well, ye whose knowledge of "many exterior matters," as the mystery of punch-mixing and the like, is at present your sole boast and glory! Ah! think upon the Purgatorial Realm, wherein is no punch; wherein what spirits there are must perforce form an amalgam, not with sugar and hot water, but with phosphorus and hot sulphur! And consider, while consider you may, whether it may not be worth making some slight sacrifice of the comforts of your Soulish Man here, to escape from the necessity of being hereafter condemned to wander in the shape of your Ghostial Man, to and fro in miserable darkness, helpless, restless, guideless; with that *Accusing Numeral* for ever before your eyes, and legions of black and darkest-grey spectres for ever making mockery of your most forlorn and doloriferous condition!

"The Three Half Crowns" is a review of a sonnet sequence written by Gian Battista Casti on the subject of his debt in that amount. In his review, Mangan quotes with enthusiasm a series of the sonnets covering the author's growing mania as his creditor duns him for this insignificant debt. Although an English translation of *I Tré Giuli* by Montagu Montagu had been published in London in 1826 and reappeared in 1841, Mangan has made up his own versions, and the review becomes simply a *tour de force*, in which Mangan quotes twenty-two sonnets, each one having a different rhyme scheme, except for three perfect Italian sonnets. Playful as the subject and his treatment of it are, there is no doubt that the sorrows of the debtor would have had some personal significance for Mangan, who was only rarely out of debt.

The most characteristic prose work by Mangan is the *pastiche*, "A Sixty Drop Dose of Laudanum," that series of sixty aphorisms, parables and jokes which reveal the lively mind of Mangan. Here, as in his poetry, humor and incisive portrayals of human nature are blended in a loose but always amusing work. Because Mangan's prose works are so long out of print, as well as for the pleasure, the quotation of a few of them is in order:

> If you desire to padlock a punster's lips never tell him that you loathe puns: he would then perpetrate his atrocities for the sake of annoying you. Choose another course: always affect to misunderstand him. When an excruciator has been inflicted on you, open wide your eyes and mouth for a minute, and then, closing them again abruptly, shake your head, and exclaim, "Very mysterious!" This kills him.

* * *

> The most opaque of all the masques that people assume to conceal their real characters is enthusiasm. In the eyes of women enthusiasm appears so amiable that they believe no impostor *could* counterfeit it: to men it seems so ridiculous that they are satisfied nobody *would*.

* * *

> No neglect, no slight, no contumely from one of his own sex can mortify a man who has been much flattered and courted by women. No matter from what source it may emanate, he will always and necessarily attribute it to envy.

* * *

Writing a poem for the sake of developing a meta-
physical theory, is like kindling a fire for the sake of the
smoke.

Mangan's prose now seems very much the product
of its time; in its stylistic peculiarities, its mixture of
wild humor with mysterious happenings, and particularly in its insistent moral tone, the prose reminds us
of Carlyle's *Sartor Resartus*. Like his Scottish contemporary, Mangan shows a keen perception of human
folly and social injustice. Of course, the Irish writer
is more playful and less systematic in his exposition,
and he has left no major work of prose comparable to
so many of Carlyle's.

One composition in prose does rank with the best
of his poetry: his *Autobiography*, which is, unfortun-
ately, incomplete. But in that work, Mangan's skill as a
prose writer is undeniable: he evokes vivid pictures
and expresses strong convictions in an unusual but
haunting style. The account of his early years there
presented is as artistic as any of his lyric poems, and
the conviction of his own doom, as well as the equally
strong belief in God's providence, unifies even the
autobiographical fragment so that it becomes more
than merely a source of biographical information, but
an integral and artistic work.

No more extended summary of the significance of
the life and writings of James Clarence Mangan is
needed than the tributes printed in *The Nation* shortly
after his death:

He has faults, which he who runs may read, mannerism,
grotesque, and an indomitable love of jinglng; he often

sins against simplicity, but the inexpiable sin of commonplace no man can lay to his charge.

* * *

It is enough . . . to say that Mangan, a man of great gifts and great attainments, lived a pauper and a drudge, and died in a hospital. To most he was but a voice which has now ceased for ever . . . . To death he had long looked forward.

Selected Bibliography

EDITIONS:

Poems of James Clarence Mangan, ed. D. J. O'Donoghue.
  Dublin: M. H. Gill & Son, Ltd., 1903.
The Prose Writings of James Clarence Mangan, ed. D. J.
  O'Donoghue. Dublin: M. H. Gill & Son, Ltd., 1904.
The Autobiography of James Clarence Mangan, ed. James
  Kilroy. Dublin: Dolmen Press, 1968.
Anthologia Germanica. Dublin: W. Curry, 1845.
The Poets and Poetry of Munster; verse translations by
  J. C. Mangan. Dublin, John O'Daly, 1849.
Poems by James Clarence Mangan, ed. John Mitchel. New
  York: P. M. Haverty, 1859.
James Clarence Mangan, His Selected Poems; with a Study,
  ed. Imogen Guiney. London: John Lane, 1897.

BIBLIOGRAPHY:

P. S. O'Hegarty, *A Bibliography of James Clarence Mangan*.
  Dublin: Alex Thom & Co., Ltd., 1941.
Rudi Holzapfel, "Mangan's Poetry in the *Dublin University
  Magazine*: a Bibliography," *Hermathena*. January, 1968.

BIOGRAPHY:

D. J. O'Donoghue, *The Life and Writings of James Clarence
  Mangan*. Edinburgh: P. Geddes, 1897.

CRITICAL STUDIES:

Henry Edward Cain, *James Clarence Mangan and the Poe-Mangan Question*. Doctoral dissertation for Catholic University of America. 1929.

James Joyce, "James Clarence Mangan," *St. Stephen's*. May, 1902.

Francis Thompson, "James Clarence Mangan," *Academy*. 25 September 1897.

————, "Mangan the Unhappy," *Academy*. 15 August 1903.

————, "A Bewildered Poet," *Academy*. 16 May 1903.

Francis J. Thompson, "Poe and Mangan, 1949," *Dublin Magazine*. January, 1950.

————, "Mangan in America," *Dublin Magazine*. July, 1952.

W. B. Yeats, "Clarence Mangan's Love Affair," *United Ireland*. 22 August 1891.

Rudi Holzapfel, *James Clarence Mangan: A Check List of Printed and other Sources*. Dublin: Scepter Publishers Ltd., 1969.